This book belongs to

....

....

Spot's
Storybook

Eric Hill

FREDERICK WARNE

Contents

Spot's
First Picnic

Spot was going on his first picnic with his friends, Tom, Helen and Steve, and he was very excited. He squeezed three jam sandwiches into his backpack.
"I hope I haven't forgotten anything," said Spot as he licked his sticky paws.

Then he had an idea.
"Just what we need for our picnic!" shouted Spot.
And before Sally could stop him, Spot had pulled the
tablecloth off the table – and everything with it. *Crash!*

A knock at the door saved Spot from getting
into more trouble.
"Your friends are here, Spot," Sally called.
Spot rushed to the door.
"Let's go," said Spot.
"Bye, Mum!"
Sally looked up at
the sky. It was cloudy.
"Be careful," she told
them. "And come back
if it rains."
"Don't worry,"
said Helen.
"I'll be in charge."

They climbed up a hill and Spot
pointed to a small wood on the
other side.
"Let's go there," he said.
"I know where there's a stream
and a big tree we can sit under for
our picnic. Come on. I'll race you
to the stream!"

Spot got there first. Steve was second and Helen came in third. Tom panted up last, but when he saw the water, he was the first one in. *Splash!*

"It was silly of you to jump in like that, Tom," Helen scolded. "You might have hurt yourself."

"Sorry," said Tom. "But I'm fine now. Let's go and eat."

Spot, Helen and Steve crossed the stream on stepping stones.

Spot put down the tablecloth and Helen unpacked the food.
They had just started to eat when it began to rain.
"Quick, everyone," Helen shouted. "Put the tablecloth over
the branch and make a tent."

It was cosy and dry under the tablecloth, but Steve stayed outside.

"It's only a shower," he said, as he climbed up on a branch. Suddenly Spot heard Steve shout, "Ooops!" and the tent began to shake. Then everything went dark.

Steve had slipped off the branch and pulled the tent down on top of everyone.

"That's the end of our picnic," moaned Spot.

"It's all your fault, Steve," Helen complained.

"You and your silly monkey tricks."

"We may as well go home," said Spot.

They packed up and started back across the stream. But the stones were slippery from the rain and Helen lost her balance. "Help!" she cried. They all tried to catch Helen, but she fell and pulled everyone into the water with her.

What a mess! Spot looked around and laughed.
"That was your fault, Helen. You and your silly
balancing tricks!"
Everyone started giggling, and Helen laughed too.
"Wait until Mum sees us," Spot said.

But Sally had a surprise ready for them when they got home. "I knew you'd come back wet and hungry so I made you an indoor picnic."
"Thanks, Mum!" said Spot. "We are starving. We didn't mind getting wet at all, but we did mind eating soggy sandwiches!"

Spot
Finds a Key

Spot was playing in the garden. He saw something shining on the garden path.
"What's that?" he said. "It's a key!"
"Perhaps it's a key to the garden shed," said a bird.

"Let's see," said Spot. He tried to put the key in the lock of the garden shed but it was too small.

"Dad might know where this key comes from," said Spot. "Here he is. I'll ask him." But Sam was in a hurry. "Sorry, Spot, I can't stop now. I'm looking for something."

"Oh well," said Spot, "I'll try indoors. Perhaps it's the key to Mum's jewellery box."

Spot tried the key in the lock of Sally's jewellery box but it was too big.
"I'll ask Mum," said Spot. "Mum, do you know what..."
Sally didn't stop to listen. "Sorry, Spot, I must go and help Dad. I'll be back in a minute."

"Perhaps it's the key to the desk," thought Spot. He tried to put the key in the lock of the desk. The key was the right size but it wouldn't turn.

"This game is fun. Where else shall I try? Perhaps it's the key to the kitchen cupboard."

He put the key in the lock of the cupboard. It was the right size and it turned the lock, but it didn't open the cupboard.

"Oh," said Spot, disappointed.
"What else can there be?
Hello, I wonder why Dad's
left his toolbox on the floor?
Now that's got a lock..."

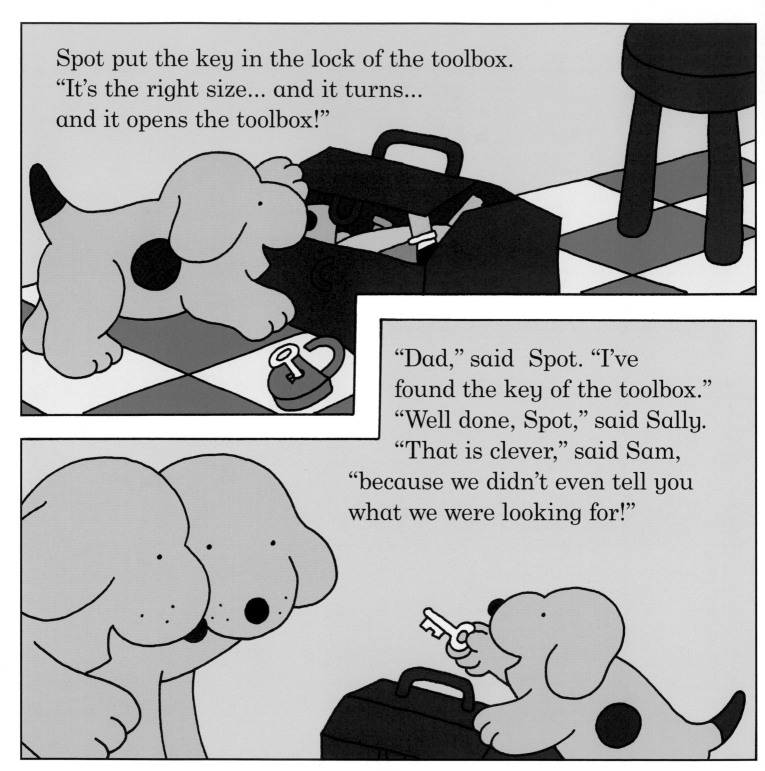

Spot put the key in the lock of the toolbox.
"It's the right size... and it turns...
and it opens the toolbox!"

"Dad," said Spot. "I've found the key of the toolbox."
"Well done, Spot," said Sally.
"That is clever," said Sam, "because we didn't even tell you what we were looking for!"

Spot's Favourite Toy

Spot and Tom were in the garden playing with Spot's ball.
"I think my ball is my favourite toy," said Spot.

Just then it started to rain.
"Let's go indoors," said Spot. "Mum, can we play indoors?"
"Of course," said Sally. "But you can't play with
the ball inside the house, Spot. You'll have to find
another toy to play with."

Spot and Tom went to Spot's room.
Spot picked up his train.
"Now *this* is my
favourite toy,"
he said.

Tom was looking in the
toy box. He found
Spot's cars.
"Can we play with the
cars, Spot?" he asked.
"They're my favourite."

28

"Mine too," said Spot. "Come on, let's race them."
Spot's car won the first race, Tom's car won the
second race, and in the third race the cars went
so fast that they hit the cupboard with a big bang.
"Mind the furniture, boys!" called Sally.

"I've got to go now," said Tom.
"See you tomorrow, Spot."
Spot was sorry to see Tom leave.

"Now what shall I play
with?" thought Spot when
Tom had gone.
"I know, my building bricks."

"Helen's here," called Sally.
"Hello, Helen," said Spot. "Help me build a tower with my building bricks. They're my favourite toy."
"Mine too," said Helen. "Let's see how high we can make it."

As Helen placed her brick on top, the tower wobbled. Spot tried to hold it. *Crash!* Spot and Helen and the bricks landed on the floor in a heap.

"It's time to go," said Helen. "Bye, Spot."

"It's bath time, Spot," said Sally.
"That's good," said Spot. "I can play with my boat. It's my favourite toy."
"After your bath you must put all your toys away before you go to bed."

So Spot had his bath and tidied his toys away and went to bed.

"Did you put all your toys away, Spot?" asked Sally.
"Yes, Mum. All except Teddy. He's in bed with me. He really *is* my favourite toy."

Spot's Hospital Visit

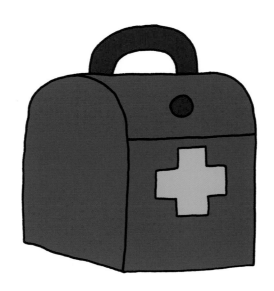

"I'm ready!" Spot shouted to Tom and Helen. They were all going to visit Steve, who was in hospital with a broken leg.

Tom had a ball for Steve, and Helen was taking her doctor's bag and a big bunch of flowers. She was pushing them in her dolls' pushchair. Spot had a basket full of fruit.
"These are for Steve," said Spot.
"We'd better hurry or there won't be any left!" said Helen.

At the hospital, they found Steve's room. Steve waved.
"Thank you for coming," he called. "I love visitors,
especially when they bring me presents!"
Spot looked at the plaster cast on Steve's leg.
"Doesn't that hurt?" he asked.
"Not at all," said Steve. "Anyway, it's coming off tomorrow."

"There's writing on your cast," said Spot.
Steve laughed. "Yes, the doctors and nurses have written their names on my leg."
"I want to write my name," said Spot. So he did, and then Tom drew a funny face. Helen wrote her name and drew some flowers and a heart.

Tom was looking at Steve's hospital bed. There was a handle at the side.
"What's this for?" he asked as he started to turn it.
Steve's head and shoulders rose into the air.
"Hey! Look at that!" shouted Tom.

Spot found another handle on the other side of the bed and began turning. Steve's feet went up.
"Be careful!" Steve yelled. "You're not supposed to do that. I might break something else!"

Suddenly the door opened and Nurse Rabbit came in with a wheelchair.
"Here Steve," she said. "Why don't you take your friends to the playroom?" They went along the corridor.

"Look at all these toys," said Tom.
"I like this train," said Spot.
Helen opened her doctor's bag and took out a green mask and gown.

"Let's play doctor," she said. "You're my patient, Tom."
So Tom sat down and Helen listened to his chest.
He began to laugh and twist around.
"Sit still!" Helen ordered. "You don't laugh and fool around
when a real doctor examines you."
"But you're tickling me," giggled Tom.

"Let's pretend Spot has broken his leg," said Helen.
She unrolled a bandage and wound it around Spot's leg.
"Put Spot in your pushchair, Helen!" shouted Steve.
"Tom, look at Spot." But Tom wasn't there.

Helen wheeled Spot into the hall and Steve wheeled himself out in the wheelchair.

"Where can Tom be?" he asked. They went down the corridor calling out Tom's name. But he was nowhere in sight.

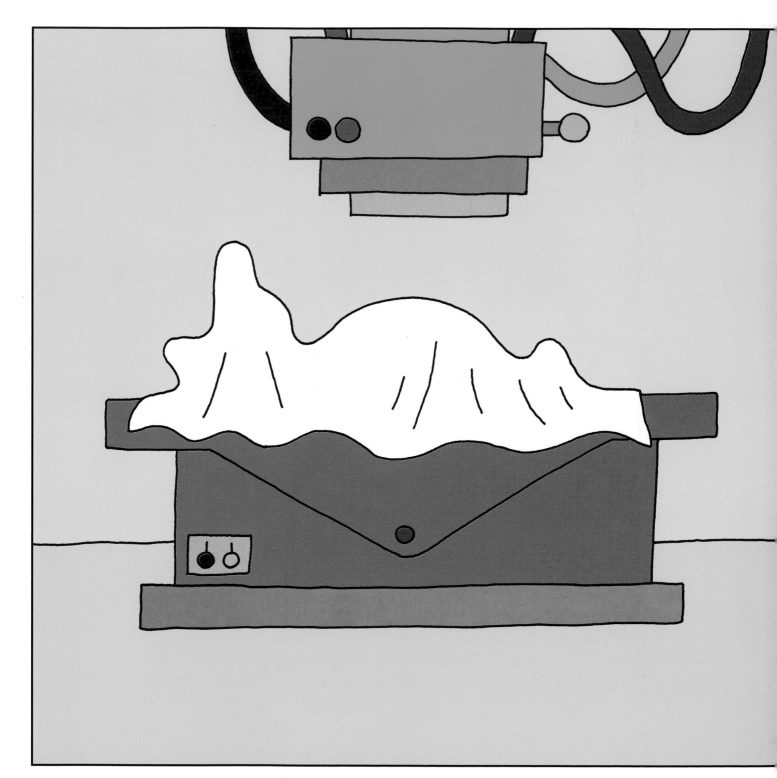

They looked in the X-ray room.
"This is the machine that took pictures
of my leg," Steve told them.
"I know about X-ray machines," said
Helen. "They're like cameras, but they
take pictures of your bones."
"I don't see Tom in here," said Steve.
"Do you?"

As the three friends turned around to leave, a loud voice shouted, "BOO!" They all jumped.
There sat Tom. He'd been hiding under a sheet all the time.
"Did I scare you?" he laughed.

Visiting time was over, so they said goodbye to Steve and went back to Spot's house. Helen wheeled Spot with his bandaged leg all the way in her pushchair. Sally was at the door as they arrived.

"Spot!" she cried. "What happened to your leg?"

"Don't worry," Spot told her. "Helen was just playing doctor."

"I liked the hospital," said Spot. "We had fun. I think I'd like to be a doctor when I grow up."

"Maybe you will," said Sally. "But in the meantime, Steve will soon be out of the hospital, and you can all play doctor at home."

"Great!" said Spot.

Spot
Goes Splash!

It was raining when Spot woke up.
"Oh dear," he thought. "I'll have to stay indoors. I wonder what Steve and Helen are doing today?"
"Breakfast is ready," Sally called from the kitchen.
Spot loved breakfast. He forgot all about the rain.

After he had finished eating, Spot looked
outside again.
"Oh good," he said. "It's stopped raining.
Can I go outside and play, Mum?"
"All right," Sally told him. "But don't
get all wet and muddy. I've just cleaned
the house before Grandma and Grandpa
come to visit."

Spot went out into the garden. The sun was beginning
to shine. Spot saw Steve looking up at the sky.
"Do you see the rainbow, Spot?" asked Steve.
"Yes!" said Spot. "It's so many
different colours."

Helen came along wearing a raincoat, a big rain hat and shiny red wellington boots.
"It's stopped raining, Helen," said Spot
"I know," said Helen.

"You don't need your raincoat and hat and boots any more,"
Steve told her.
"Yes I do," said Helen, smiling. "Especially the boots. I need
them to walk through puddles. Like this..."
And she stamped through a big puddle. Splash!

"That looks like fun!" said Spot.
"Let's try it!" said Steve. And they splashed through the puddles too, stamping and shouting.
"You two are silly," said Helen. "Now your feet are all wet and muddy."
"We don't care," they said. "This is great!"

"It's starting to rain again," said Helen. "I'm still nice and dry, and you two will have to go home."
"I suppose so," said Spot, having one last splash.

By the time he got home, Spot was
very wet and very muddy.
Sally was not pleased.
"Get into the bath at once," she said.
"But it's not time to go to bed yet,"
said Spot.
"I know," said Sally, "but it's time
for a bath."

So Spot got into the bath with his boat and toy duck. "This is fun too," he thought. "But after this I think I've had enough water for one day."

Spot
goes to the Fair

Grandma and Grandpa took Spot to the fair. "What would you like to go on first, Spot?"
"I'd like to go on the merry-go-round," said Spot. "Please."
Grandpa lifted Spot up on to the horse. "You too, Grandma and Grandpa," said Spot.

"This is fun,"
Grandpa said.
Grandma agreed.
"Ooh, I can't
remember when
I last did this."

"What next, Spot?" asked Grandma.
Spot looked around.
"I'd like to go on the helter-skelter," he said.

Spot came whizzing down.
"*Wheee!*"
"I'd like to go on that," said Grandpa.
"Me too," said Grandma.

Grandma came down the slide followed
by Grandpa.
"This is great, Spot. What a time
we're having!"
Spot laughed to see his grandparents
having so much fun. Then he went on
the helter-skelter again.

"Can I go on the bumper cars now?" Spot asked.
"I'll sit with you," said Grandma.
"I'll just watch," said Grandpa. A loud buzz started and Spot pushed down on the pedal. They were off.

"There's Helen and Tom! Hold tight, Grandma," shouted
Spot, as Helen bumped her car into theirs. *Bang!*
"My word," said Grandma, "this is some ride!"

Then Spot bumped
Helen's car.
"That's the fun of it,"
said Spot, laughing.
Bang!

69

When the ride finished, Spot and Grandma climbed out of the car.
"That was a bit scary," said Grandma.
"It was," said Spot, "but sometimes it's fun to be a bit scared."

"Where's Grandpa?" asked Grandma.
He was nowhere in sight.
Suddenly Helen pointed. "I think I can see him.
He's carrying something big and pink."

"Where have you been?" said Grandma. "We were worried."
"I got bored waiting so I tried my luck on the coconut shy.
I won this for Spot."
"Wow!" said Spot, as he licked the candyfloss Grandpa had
bought. "You are clever."
It was time to go.
"Thanks for a lovely fun day," said Spot.
"Thank *you*, Spot," said Grandpa. "We enjoyed it
as much as you did."

Sweet Dreams, Spot

It was the start of a busy day. After breakfast, Spot went with his mum to do the shopping. There was a long list of things to get.

"Thank you, Spot," said Sally. "I couldn't have done all this without your help."

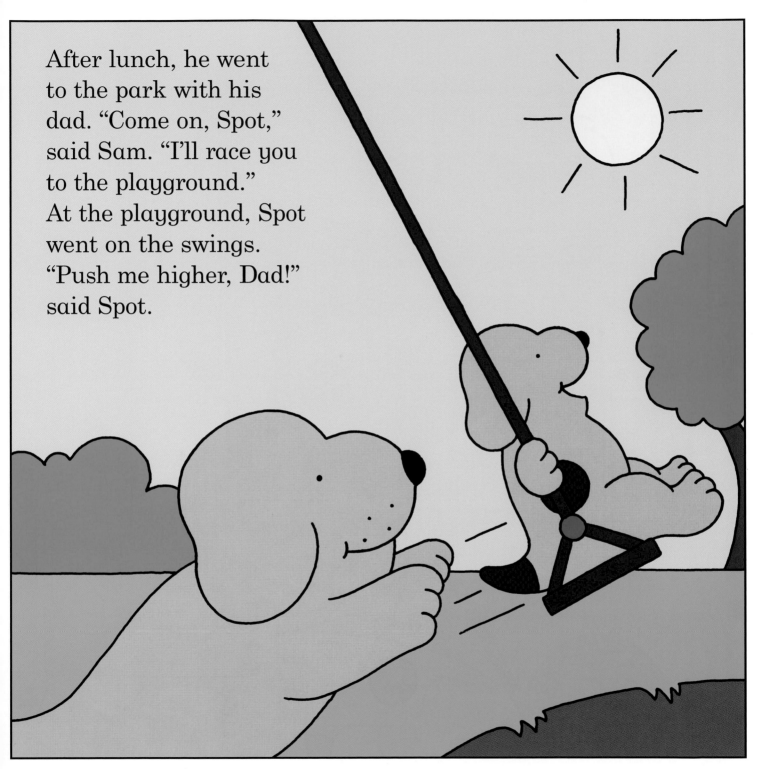

After lunch, he went to the park with his dad. "Come on, Spot," said Sam. "I'll race you to the playground." At the playground, Spot went on the swings. "Push me higher, Dad!" said Spot.

When Spot and his dad got home from the park, Helen, Tom and Steve came over to play hide-and-seek.

Finally, as it was getting dark, Spot's friends went home to bed.
Spot was ready for bed too.

After Spot had eaten his supper, he went
for a last walk in the garden.
"Hello, Spot," a small voice said,
"Have you come out to play?"
"No, I'm going to bed," said Spot.
"Oh well," said the mole,
"sleep tight."

As Spot walked by the pond, he heard a frog croak.
"Hello, Spot. It's a lovely evening for a swim."
"Not for me, thanks. I'm off to bed," said Spot.

"Tu-whit tu-whoo!" hooted the owl.
"Goodnight, Owl," said Spot.
"What do you mean *goodnight*?"
the owl asked. "I've just woken up.
I've got lots to do."
"Rather you than me," Spot yawned.
"I've had a busy day."

Spot went back indoors.
"Goodnight, everyone," he said.
"Have fun!" Spot kissed his dad.
"I've had a lovely day, Dad. Thanks for taking me to the park."
"Goodnight, Spot," said Sam.

Sally came in to kiss Spot goodnight.
"Please read me a story, Mum," said Spot.
Sally opened the book and started to read.

Spot snuggled down.
He got sleepier and sleepier.
By the time the story was
over, Spot was fast asleep.

"What a tired little puppy you were," Sally whispered.
"I've been reading the story and there was no
one listening."
"Oh yes there was," said a voice. Sally looked around and there
were the owl, the frog and the mole.
"Thanks for the story, Sally," they said. "Sweet dreams, Spot."
Spot opened one eye.
"Yes, thanks, Mum," he said.
"Goodnight, everyone."
And he fell fast asleep again.

Spot's Windy Day

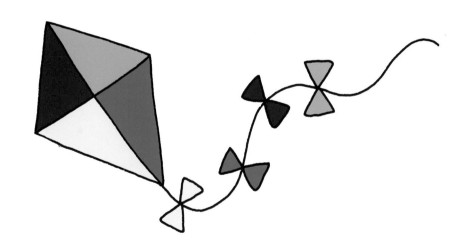

One windy day, Spot went out to fly his kite.
"See you later, Mum," he called to Sally.
"Don't get blown away, Spot!" said Sally.
Spot ran up and down the field with
his kite, trying to get the wind to
lift it up into the air. Suddenly
a strong gust caught the kite.
"Oh!" Spot cried. "Look how high it is!"

Then, "Oops!" said Spot. "How did that happen?" His kite had landed in a tree. Spot looked up at it. "I can't reach up there," he said. "That's the end of flying my kite. Oh no!"

Spot started to walk home. He was a little sad.
Leaves were blowing all around him in the wind.
Red, yellow, green and orange ones.

"I'll try and catch a leaf," he said. But it was harder than he thought. As soon as one came near him, the wind whisked it away again. Spot looked up and saw something big and dark above him. "Ooh!" Spot said, reaching up. "What's that?"

It blew here and there. It came lower and lower – and *whoosh* – it landed right on Spot's head and covered his eyes.

Spot couldn't see anything.
But he heard a voice say,
"Well, well, there's my hat!"
Spot pulled on the sides of the hat
and someone pulled on the front.
Pop! Off came the hat and Spot found
himself looking up at Mr Kangaroo.

"Thank you, Spot. You saved my best Sunday hat!"
"It was nothing," said Spot.
"I wish I could do something for you, Spot!"
said Mr Kangaroo.

"You can!" said Spot. "My kite is
stuck up in the tree. Can you
reach it?"

90

"Certainly," said Mr Kangaroo.
He jumped up and knocked the kite
down to the ground.
"Wow!" said Spot.
"I'm glad your hat
found me!"

Spot's kite once again soared up in the sky.
"Thank you, Mr Kangaroo!" shouted Spot.
But Mr Kangaroo couldn't hear.
It was too windy.

Spot
Follows his Nose

One morning, Spot went out for a walk. He stopped and sniffed.
"What smells so nice?" he asked. Spot went to the flowers in the garden. He sniffed.
"No. That's not what I can smell," he said.

His friend Helen came by on her bike.
"Hello, Spot. Why are you sniffing?"
"I can smell something really nice," Spot said, "but I don't know what it is."

"Mr Kangaroo has just cut his grass," said Helen. "Maybe that's what you can smell." Spot ran across to Mr Kangaroo's house.

"Hey, Spot!" Mr Kangaroo shouted. "What are you doing with my pile of grass?"
"I was only sniffing at it," said Spot. "But it's not the smell I'm looking for."

Next door, Tom was painting the fence in front of his house.
"I wonder if it's the paint I can smell?" said Spot.
He went up to the fence and sniffed.
"That smells awful!"

Tom laughed. "You've got paint on your nose!"
Spot rubbed his nose.
"I have to go home now," he told Tom.

As Spot went up the path to his house, the smell got stronger.
He ran inside. Sally was polishing a table in the hall.
Spot jumped up and sniffed at the table top.
"You've put your dirty paws all over my
nice clean table!" cried Sally.
"I'm sorry, Mum," said Spot.
"I've been smelling something nice
all morning. But this isn't it."

"Why don't you look in the kitchen, Spot?"
said Sally.
Spot ran to the kitchen.
"That's the smell!" he shouted.
There on the table was a plate of hot cookies.

"I baked these for later," Sally told him. "But you can have one now." She smiled. "There's nothing wrong with your sense of smell, Spot!"

"No," said Spot. "And there's nothing wrong with my sense of taste either. Thanks for the cookies, Mum!"

Spot
in the Snow

One morning, Spot woke up and got a big surprise. Outside, everything was covered in snow.

"Mum, can I go out with my sledge?" Spot asked.

"Yes, but put on your hat and scarf," said Sally. "It's very cold outside."

"I don't need all that, Mum," said Spot, opening the door. "Brrr! You're right, Mum. It *is* cold."

Spot put on his hat and scarf.

By the time Spot had pulled his sledge to the top of the hill, he was feeling warm again. He sat on his sledge and pushed himself off. *Whoosh!* Down he went to the bottom of the hill. "This is great!" he said.

Steve was skating on the pond.
"Hello, Spot!" Steve called out.
"Do you want to try my skates?"

Skating looked easy when Steve did it. But Spot found it wasn't so easy after all.
"I think I'll stick with my sledge. Come and ride with me, Steve."

They climbed the hill, pulling the sledge together. When they reached the top they got on the sledge.

"Ready, steady... go!"

The sledge went much faster with Spot and Steve both on it.

"*Whee!* This is fantastic!" shouted Steve.

"Yes," cried Spot. "Watch out for the... Oh!"

The sledge hit a big pile of snow and came to a sudden stop.
Spot and Steve rolled out into the snow.
Then something knocked Spot's hat down over his eyes.
"What's that?" Spot asked.
They heard giggling, and there was Helen, laughing at
them all covered in snow.
"It's a snowball," she called. "And here's another!"
And before he could move, a big squishy
snowball hit Steve in the tummy.

"Here's one for you!" yelled Steve, throwing a snowball back.
"And another!" shouted Spot.
"Hey!" said Helen. "Two against one isn't fair. Come and help me build a snowman. Look, I've already started."

Helen had rolled a big snowball for the snowman's body.
Spot helped her roll another one for his head.
"Come and help us, Steve," called Spot.
"In a minute," said Steve. "I'm busy."

Helen and Spot put the head on the body. They found two stones for the snowman's eyes and a piece of wood for his mouth.
"Look at our snowman, Steve," called Spot.
"And look at what I've made," said Steve.

Steve had made a "snowdog" on top of Spot's sledge.
It looked a lot like Spot.
"That's great!" said Spot. "Why did you build it on my sledge?"
"So you could take it home, Spot."
"Mum will be surprised when two Spots come home,"
said Spot. "It's lucky she told me to wear my hat and scarf so she'll know which is me!"

Spot
Tidies Up

Spot and Steve had been playing all day and Spot's bedroom was a mess.
"Vroom," said Spot, as he pushed a car along the floor.
"Coming in to land!" said Steve, holding an aeroplane high up in the air.

Spot's mum looked in.

"What a fine time you've had! But it's time to tidy up now."

"OK, Mum," said Spot, with one last push on the car.

"I'll help," said Steve.

Steve put the aeroplane back in the toy box with the boat and train set.

119

All the books went back in the bookcase and the rest of the toys went into the cupboard.
"There! All done!" said Spot. "Thanks for your help, Steve."

After Steve had gone home, Spot got ready for bed. "What a fun day I've had," he thought, as he brushed his teeth. "And I've got a nice clean, tidy room."

Spot was just about to climb into his basket when he noticed something was missing. He looked around the room. "Where's Teddy?"

Spot ran to his toy box. One by one, he sorted through the toys. Teddy wasn't there.

Spot went to the bookcase. Maybe Teddy was hidden behind a book? But he wasn't. Spot looked inside the cupboard. No Teddy.

Sally came in to say goodnight. "I thought you had tidied up your room, Spot," she said.
"I did, Mum, but I can't find my teddy," said Spot.
"I'll help you," said Sally. "Have you looked in your basket?"

125

Spot rushed to his basket and lifted the cushion.
"I've found Teddy! Thanks, Mum. I promise to tidy up again in the morning."
"I know you will," smiled Sally.
She tucked Spot up with Teddy and whispered,
"Goodnight, Spot. Goodnight, Teddy. Sweet dreams."

Spot Plays
Hide-and-Seek

Spot was playing in his bedroom when he had an idea.
"I want to play hide-and-seek," he said. He took all the toys
out of his toy box and climbed inside. After a moment,
Spot looked out.
"I need someone to find me," he said.
Spot climbed out and
ran downstairs.

Spot's mum was in the kitchen as Spot ran by. He saw
a laundry basket.
"Ah, that's a good place to hide," he said.
He jumped in just as Sally walked past.

"Boo!" said Spot.
Sally turned round and laughed.
"I didn't see you, Spot," she said.
"Good. Will you play hide-and-seek with me?" asked Spot.
"All right," said Sally. "We can play in the garden."

"I'm playing hide-and-seek with my mum," said Spot to the rabbit.
"You're too big to hide in here," said the rabbit.

Sally looked behind the bushes.
She looked in the vegetable patch.

She looked over the wall.
"Where can Spot be hiding?" said Sally.
"Not here," said the goose.

Spot heard Sally coming. "Hide behind the tree," said the squirrel. "I won't tell."

Sally walked past the tree and
went to the shed.
"Look out, Spot," she called,
"I'm coming to find you."

Spot wasn't in the shed.
"I don't know where Spot can be,"
said Sally. "Perhaps he has gone
back to the house to hide."

Spot's dad came along and picked up the wheelbarrow.
"Have you seen Spot?" asked Sally.
"No," said Sam.

"Hi, Dad," said Spot standing up.
"I've been hiding from Mum."
"Yes, Spot, I know," said Sam.
"She has gone back to the house
to look for you."

"I think I've done enough hiding," said Spot.
"I'll go back too." As he got to the house,
Spot heard his mum call out, "Steve is here,
Spot. He wants to play."

"Hello Spot," said Steve. "Do you want to play
Hide-and-seek?" Spot thought for a moment.
"OK," said Spot, "But only if you hide and I seek."
"Great," said Steve.

Spot started to count as Steve ran off
to hide.
"Good luck, Steve," said Sally.
"If Spot seeks as well as he hides,
it will be a short game!"

FREDERICK WARNE
Published by the Penguin Group
Penguin Books Ltd, 80 Strand, London WC2R 0RL, England
Penguin Books Australia Ltd,
250 Camberwell Road, Camberwell, Victoria 3124, Australia
New York, Canada, India, New Zealand, South Africa
First published by Frederick Warne 2005
This edition published 2012
10 9 8 7 6 5 4 3 2 1
Copyright © Eric Hill, 2005
Eric Hill has asserted his moral rights under
the Copyright, Designs and Patents Act of 1988
All rights reserved
ISBN 978 0 72326 967 0
Planned and produced by Ventura Publishing Ltd
80 Strand, London WC2R 0RL
Printed in China